Dedicated to the author's lifelong commitment

M.D. Tophus

Victims of Crime: Introduction to Forensic Challenges in Healthcare.

Hilphma Publications 2022. www.hilphmapublication.com

First Edition.

Germany.

The author has over 25 years of clinical experience in the healthcare field. Is cognisant of both DSM-5-TR (and previous versions) and ICD-11 (and previous versions) disorders and conditions; quality and safety improvement in healthcare; and healthcare education.

Victims of crime are often not uniquely known to police, courts, or other judicial branches. They invariably become known to healthcare providers (whether psychologists, psychiatrists, rehabilitation workers, physiotherapists, or specialist medical providers). This can be for injuries sustained, or for general medical/therapeutic treatment related (and unrelated) to their victim status.

Departmental corruption, criminal offending, social media crime, mainstream crimes (including homicides), institutional power based crimes, and those associated with disclosure and whistleblowing are all highly relevant to the healthcare worker's professional path.
For where there appears one, or many, of the above variants of victims of crime, comes tasks with which one is not so familiar, processes which are blurred and contacts less accessible.
Ultimately, without some knowledge, experience, or at least stimulated know-how, when it comes to victims of crime, the healthcare worker becomes very much an island, left to fend for themselves, and create processes of which they are unsure, and which are informalised.

The following publication introduces the concepts of forensic thinking, process, and implementation, to a wide variety of realistic applications in healthcare service provision.
It includes guidance, prompts, exemplifications for review, considerations, initial profiling, discussion requiring direct response, along with specific questions for research, and for application directly to departmental/private functionality realms.
In a nutshell: explanation, explication, exemplification, and direct questioning, forensically, regarding victims of crime presenting to healthcare professionals.

Other M.D. Tophus publications available:

"Exercising Quality in Healthcare Service Provision: A Complex Care Workbook for All Healthcare Professionals." Hilphma Publications: 2022.

"Who is This Colleague?: Dangers of the Healthcare Profession, and beyond. An Interview Guide for Recruitment, Performance Appraisal and Post-Adverse Events."
Hilphma Publications: 2022.

"Think on your Feet: Those Who Can. For the Consummate Healthcare Professional."
Hilphma Publications: 2022.

"The Unfortunate Healthcare Treater, The Hapless Healthcare Therapist: Narcissistic and Borderline Personality Disorder clients. The Grit."
Hilphma Publications: 2022.

CONTENTS

The *Victims of Crime UN Declaration*: describes "victims" as the following: "who, individually or collectively, have suffered harm, including physical or mental injury, emotional suffering, economic loss or substantial impairment of their fundamental rights, through acts or omissions that are in violation of criminal laws...including those laws prescribing criminal abuse of power" (1).
Furthermore, "A person may be considered a victim..regardless of whether the perpetrator is identified, apprehended, prosecuted...and regardless of the familial relationship between the perpetrator and the victim" (1).

Moreover, in the *UK Victim's Code*, 'a "victim" is: ..a close relative (or a nominated family spokesperson) of a person whose death was directly caused by a criminal offence" (2).

Examples of victimisation are: hate crime, bias crime, crime committed with "a discriminatory motive", "..whether the offender was in a position of control" (3).

One of the directives for *victims of terrorism*, is to 'protect their dignity and security' (4); and including the family members of victims.

In **Europe, and in many other regions**, victim support exists. This is necessary, especially, for protective measures regarding intimidation and retaliation (by perpetrator/s) during criminal investigations and court proceedings. <u>Protection from repeat victimisation perpetrated by secondary persons is integral to this.</u>

Victims often experience victim blaming and victim shaming.
Interventions include specialist support services; trauma care; ensuring the victim's psychological integrity; and, assistance in power re-balancing.

Of particular relevance are the aspects of: 'liberty and security, respect for private and family life', 'physical and mental integrity', 'the principle of non discrimination'; 'equality between men and women', with focus upon the 'right to dignity' (5).

When someone is being victimised, likewise interventions such as the **U.S.A.'s** DOJ 'No fear act' discrimination and whistleblower protection laws (2006), is vital.

The following chapters fully embrace the notion of departmental corruption. The first chapter, in particular, includes law enforcement as exemplification of how departmental corruption can easily become extensive, and ultimately- with far-reaching consequences. It is quintessentially, Police; Silencing; in relation to computer hacking and Stalking victim.

The second chapter, Fraud; Forgery; and Injustice in the counselling room.

The third chapter, Risk of mistaken identity; and alleged culpability/alert to presumption of guilt when taping for evidence.

The fourth related chapter, Case of Subterfuge; Disappearance; False identity regarding children.

The fifth chapter, moves focus to criminal offender Profiling.

The sixth chapter, integrates Social media offences: revenge, hate crimes, bias crimes, and the effects which can lead to cultism.

The seventh and eighth chapters, cover mainstream crimes, such as physical, sexual, assaults and homicides.

The ninth through to tenth chapters, examine institutional power based crimes. That of religious movements, and politically oriented ones.

The final chapters (eleven through thirteen) encompass disclosure and whistleblowing, with the equally important specifications of: endemic, healthcare abuses, along with paedophile rings.

DEPARTMENTAL CORRUPTION: Police; Silencing; Stalking victim

CORRUPTION in POLICING: Summary:

> *-Enclaves, where slowly, accepted norms and principles are supplanted.*
>
> *-This can be displayed in a myriad of ways- including 'making a quick buck'; bribery; but the essential elements of corrupted thinking and behaviour (or, potential for), has to be in place firstly.*
>
> *-Reasons: deviance; internal connectedness; intrinsic and extrinsic motivators.*
>
> *-Modi: pressurisation of non-corrupt officers; 'blue brotherhood' (where loyalty knows no bounds); culture of policing/police network (eg honing in on the newly recruited)*
>
> *-Synonymous with a cult, as it has the essential elements of: covertness; specific code words; seclusion; and boundless collegial allegiances.*

One fine example of corruption:

> Not dissimilar to many domestic violence victims' experiences, who approach police officers in police stations to report a breach of an AVO.
>
> Likewise with other crimes, often, the police personnel call the perpetrator who attends the local police station, and is revealed as friends with one of the police officers.
>
> They walk out arm in arm (laughing) with the officer- in front of the victim. This happens frequently, not just in rural areas/country towns, where everyone knows everyone. In this and similar cases, the healthcare worker/s is/are often left to pick up the pieces.

Lyb approaches a federal police station.

While waiting, Lyb sights multiple police officers and personnel running out of the building.

The police statement is taken. Upon questioning of the victim the police officer reveals that he is already aware of the stalking.

The police officer tells the informant victim that the investigation will take along time, and to wait.

Other police personnel tell the victim to 'go' from the building.

The victim departs, obligingly.

The victim (thence), phones and leaves a message for a close family friend (with significant connections) residing in that particular city, and whom they had known from birth. This 'friend' later clearly acknowledged that she had received the phone message on the day of the phone call. It is unclear as to whether the friend attempted to intervene, and in which way.....

The victim changes locations (for safety reasons)- moves to a different hotel, whilst awaiting a phone call from the police officer as to the status of the investigation.

The victim receives a phone call informing them that they need to talk to the mental health crisis team who have already been contacted.

The mental health team calls the victim, and insist upon visiting the victim, the victim posed no harm to others nor themselves.

Evidence of the stalking was also available via computer hacking evidentiary documents. The mental health team states to the victim that they are 'not being stalked' (how they would have clarified this, within 2 hours is most extraordinary, in a city of over 460,000 people, with the victim being unknown within the area).

The mental health team put an <u>ultimatum to the victim, 'voluntary admission' to emergency</u> <u>for review or 'be scheduled', 'make the choice'.</u>

The <u>victim- out of fear- agrees</u> (to the former choice), the <u>victim is handcuffed</u> (with no explanation given)- with a coat placed over their arms- reasoning: 'that it is better' whilst walking through the hotel.

Upon arrival at the hospital, the 2 health personnel, start talking to Lyb about parking lots and improvements and <u>need for hospital funding</u>.

Lyb was put in a room on her own- which was <u>not part of the working area of the hospital,</u> with paint cans, and 1 other person of the opposite sex and 1 nurse. The victim had to commune in the area, for several hours, for 2 days, as part of the assessment process.

<u>Lyb was forced to undertake blood tests, a brain scan, urinalyses, and a mental health</u> <u>status exam. All of which Lyb- the victim- passed.</u>

A doctor came, the victim explained the situation, but insisted all was good, and is not being stalked (in the unit), but concerned for computer compromisation. The dr stated her <u>dislike for e-health</u>- and that due to the victim's concerns for her professional work- that her inpatient status would not be documented. This turned out (for Lyb) to become very untrue <u>(the victim lost 2 professional work careers as a result; Lyb's entire livelihood; continued to</u> <u>fear for her safety because the stalking was real- and later proven as such, and left the</u> <u>country).</u>

Lyb, without any reason given (no indication of harm, denied being stalked/fearing for safety within the hospital setting, no harm to others, passed the mental status exam), was <u>admitted to the acute psychiatric unit.</u>

<u>Lyb was released after 2 days,</u> as the doctors and rest of the healthcare team <u>could not</u> <u>justify keeping them</u> there as there was <u>no indication of mental dysfunction</u>. The victim was released without paperwork, and nil prescribed medications.
The doctors were aware that Lyb was alone, and was travelling interstate to return to their home residence.

The victim remained in the country for more than 10 months further, and then travelled to a total of 10 countries (and resided in 4 countries) and has not been known to mental health as a patient- outpatient, nor inpatient (in any arena) since (nor before) the above incident.

For those with continued interest in the above case: The following occurred inside the acute psychiatric unit:

Please read the following pages:

-Had all <u>medications</u> (essential for medical conditions and taken for over 15 years: all were non-psychiatric medications) <u>ceased</u> in the unit, immediately. Details of the victim's general practitioner were provided, and there was ample chance to make contact and verify that the medications were required.

-Mobile phone was removed from the victim, and was inaccessable for the entirety of inpatient admission.

-Admitted late in the day, there was <u>Forced medication</u> the first night (sertraline)- with the threat that it would be reported (and clear intimation of 'scheduling') if not taken willingly. This made the victim so <u>sleepy the next morning</u> that- although they were clearly required to function- socially, and interact with the other inpatients, as part of the <u>assessment process-</u> it was extremely difficult to do so.

-<u>Attempted forced medication</u> the next night with full victim/patient refusal. Upon Lyb questioning as to which medications were attempted to be given: risperidone; and 2 other anti-psychotics. The victim, upon refusal, was then (naturally) of the belief that they would be 'scheduled', and (as many patients also in the unit had stated to them, constantly, that they would not be released- whether scheduled, or not- for several months, and beyond). Lyb politely refused, the nurse stated that the victim 'must take the medications' and asked 'why' vehemently. Lyb/victim/patient responded that they felt 'it was dangerous to ingest the medications' (as in- nil proof of necessity).
The nurse laughed and left Lyb's room.

-During that night fireworks were thrown directly at the building (at the location of Lyb's room).

The victim did not leave her bed. In the morning, all other inpatients (and staff) were talking about the 'loud noises, like a bomb went off' which occured (in the early hours of the morning) and continued to do so, for many hours. The staff indicated that all other inpatients had arisen from their beds, and that they had all communed in the primary area of the unit, and had a 'good time'. They (staff and other inpatients) were all enthused by the previous night's events, and almost uncontainable in their network excitement over the events which had ensued.

-In-between these conversations, the staff approached Lyb and informed them that they must socially interact with the other inpatients (which Lyb most definitely had undertaken- constantly to that point -inspite of the shock of all the above events).

Furthermore, that Lyb must 'take the lead' and 'advocate' on behalf of mental health inpatients, in meetings (which were scheduled later in the day). In preparation (though, Lyb had done so already), the victim must walk around and interact with all inpatients in the unit, and interact, intimately. The inpatients (at this point: 1 1/4 days in the unit) with whom they had mostly interacted were: an Aboriginal elder; an 'EMO'/'Goth' young female; a patient who identified as having 'come from upstairs, from Forensics'.

In totality in the unit, Lyb discovered (and by force, interacted with) the following patient types:

-Developmentally delayed middle aged woman (with whom Lyb was expected to undertake art therapy)

-Several young groups of 'giggly', early-adulthood aged men in groups of 3.

-Domestic violence, and sexual abuse, victim with friend.

-A young suicidal female, waiting constantly for her family who never came.

-A middle aged/to older man treated as an outcast, and intimated as having internet perversion connections.

-2 loud voiced males (in late 30s and 40s age group) cajoling with clear <u>unionism-</u> speak.

-<u>Multiple other women </u>who sat together in a<u> huddle </u>in one section of the ward.

-Several others: including <u>2 young men of non- English</u> speaking background.

-After this, Lyb was forced, in mental health inpatient meetings, to be the <u>spokes-person,</u> <u>on behalf </u>of all others in the unit, to speak for their 'rights as patients'.

-In the interim (Lyb was a 'smoker of nicotine, only'), Lyb watched many other inpatients taken 'for walks'(which meant allowed to have a cigarette), taken from the unit, whilst much laughing from the staff. In this situation, one must 'earn rewards', 'show compliance', and 'earn the right for a walk/ exercise'.

-Lyb, from the first day in the unit,<u> had been requesting a meeting with doctors,</u> and other related mental health unit staff, to review the inpatient's/victim's case. At the end of 2nd day, the request was granted.

-The victim (having <u>worked in the area of mental health</u>), was fully aware of the significance of asking for this meeting. That is, <u>potential referral to the mental health</u> <u>tribunal; and/or mental health guardianship (a life-long sentence, indeed).</u>
<u>Because Lyb was not allowed access to her mobile phone, she could not contact anyone,</u> <u>including a lawyer.</u>

The parameters of the meeting were such: that Lyb must agree that Lyb <u>'is not being</u> <u>stalked' </u>(this was true in the unit, for the inpatients were only several centimetres from Lyb, at all times).

All was agreed, and Lyb signed an agreement that Lyb was not being stalked, and that they agreed to be released.

-In the interim of Lyb's release, ruddy of complexion- Caterina, an inpatient who 'had taken a liking' to the victim, and had attempted to ingratiate herself with Lyb on every occasion (since the beginning of Lyb's admission to the unit), she ('Caterina') <u>feigned a heart attack</u> <u>(ironically, or otherwise, incredibly similar to Lyb's mother's so recent death, that it was</u> <u>remarkable).</u> Lyb (with a health background) felt compelled to alert the nurses of the unit, lest the symptoms were real.

Caterina was assessed, thence sent to her room for multiple hours. She emerged very angry, and less than impressed. For she had not created the specific network that she had so desired.

-Shortly after, the victim/Lyb was released from the inpatient unit and the entire hospital, with nil recommendations for return, nor outpatient counselling (there, or in any other location), nil documentation nor psychiatric (nor related) medications.

-The original medications were handed back to Lyb (along with the mobile phone). Lyb had requested prescribing of the original medication (in order for dr's names to be recorded: the names were eventually accessed by Lyb when they requested and received all FOI documents, much later). However, the dr and team responded in the negative, as this was not allowed in an acute unit.

-To reiterate, alone; travelling by driving car interstate; and (at that point) no reports, letters, nor contact with etc to other medical treating professionals (a letter to the GP was sent 1 month later).

Infact, the inpatient's name was not printed on the patient board/nurse's board (within the unit), until permission for release was given (3 hours before release).

Choose the important forensic factors in the underlined, and between the underlined, sections of the above description. Provide comprehensive reasoning for choice of such.

Explain the human rights implications of the case. Which of the universal human rights have been compromised in this case?

It is tempting to ask, what, not who, instigated such an interrogation of 1 person?

As the victim/Lyb should have been presumed innocent, that is: victim of stalking and computer hacking (yet was handcuffed, at the insistence by the mental health staff), and was clearly mentally well, what exactly was going on?

Lyb, naturally, will never forget; never forgive each person involved; will never 'let go' of the experience, or the vast impact of not being believed nor helped, and the decimation of lifelong careers.

What would you do differently to Lyb, in such a circumstance?

DEPARTMENTAL CORRUPTION: Fraud; Forgery; and Injustice

Imagine being a victim of this: fraud; forgery; mistaken identity.

The Ultimate Nightmare: Presumption of guilt of something of which you are unaware; with no explanation from multiple populations, including close friends and family; where 'the guilt' (without the specifics) is repeated back to the victim time and time again, across multiple countries.

Sounds too bad to be true, too much in the twilight zone? Well- not necessarily.

It could be initiated by something as simple as Dania innocently signing a christmas street party application for council permission, by digitally cutting and pasting the signature (with nil encryption), in an effort for quick response, and sending the digital document (with signature accessability) to the requesting neighbour. Or one of the cases featured from this point onward:

Case of forgery and fraud:

A new client, and her partner, enter a psychology office for her first visit.

It is late in the evening, and the psychologist (Maria) is alone.

The psychology office client files are locked in a cabinet, with the file room door locked.

There is a large administration opening at chest height for client bookings and reception of clients. This area is the open partition to the client file area.

The door is alarmed/signalled for exiting and entering the building.

The client's partner waited in the waiting area, but was heard (via the signalling speaker in the psychologist's counselling room) to be coming and going (entering and exiting the building) on multiple occasions.

The psychologist, Maria, breaks the session with the client on multiple occasions to investigate.

The client's partner explains to Maria that he is going outside for a cigarette, and he will let the psychologist know if anyone else enters. There was no more signalling after this.

The signal device did have an on/off switch accessable in the waiting room.

When Maria and the client exited the counselling room, the psychologist found the client's partner again entering the building (with no signalling present).*

At the end of the session, the client pays for the session and is provided with the standard receipt signed by the psychologist, along with the psychologist's business card with the next appointment booking written on the back.

The client never returns.

Instead, the psychologist (Maria) receives a phone call from the principal psychologist of the centre asking if the psychologist had written a court report for the abovementioned client.

The answer was 'no'.

The principal psychologist was alerted to the potential falsification of the report as the letterhead was wrong (it had been copied from the receipt).

One week later, the client's lawyer makes contact with Maria asking if she, the psychologist, had written the report. Again, the answer was 'no'.

The psychologist indicated to the lawyer that they would be seeking legal advice themselves against the client, as this was forgery and fraud.

For some reason, the principal psychologist (when told of this) was upset, and vehemently dissuaded Maria from seeking legal advice, nor approaching the police (who happened to be situated directly opposite the psychology office).

Maria was a new consultant to the practice.

Maria, as the psychologist, became more and more concerned, but was reassured by the principal psychologist that nothing else would come of it...

* all of the above (please see asterisk) had to be explained in detail to the principal, that every effort was made by Maria to ensure safety protocols were adhered to- which, naturally, they were.

Both the client, and the principal psychologist, had departmental links.

Please answer the following questions:

Why was the principal psychologist reticent to report the fraud and forgery?

What may have been his reasons for questioning the treating counsellor?

Regardless of whether you work in the public, or private, arena:

Explain the step-by-step process which you have in place to protect yourself from becoming a victim of fraud and forgery?

DEPARTMENTAL CORRUPTION: Mobile phone compromisation; Risk of mistaken identity; and alert to presumption of guilt

Healthcare workers who are presented with evidence of tape recordings, require strict protocols to which are adhered, as the information may be used as evidence later.

Storage of evidence; confidentiality regarding the potential case; note-taking (of what is heard on the recording); contact with a mental health team representative/mandatory reporting of risk of harm to others (or self); and reports to the police, are integral to this.

Case of mistaken identity:

Shamu, the next door neighbour was screaming loudly, uncontrollably, and relentlessly, each day, for more than 5 years.

The extent was from morning to evening. Her screams were blood curdling.

She was alone, and would open every window and door to her house.

She would specifically stand at the window opposite the neighbour, and bellow and shriek constantly.

It could even be heard over a low flying plane.

At the 3 year mark, the neighbour made a decision, because the woman's family (who had been alerted to the problem, on multiple occasions) seemed to be doing nothing to stop it.

That is, including during holiday periods such as christmas, easter and new year (when the family would specifically depart the residence in the early morn).

The neighbour decided to start <u>taping the woman screaming</u> (which was allowed in the region in which she resided: if it was for evidence, for example court or to provide evidence to the police).

Meanwhile <u>the neighbour's phone was hacked, with all recordings also hacked.</u> This was considered potential forensic evidence.

The woman had been screaming out things in <u>5 different languages (including english), they included things like 'murder', 'terrorist', 'hate', 'f..you', and 'sl.t', etc.</u>

<u>Multiple neighbours had requested help from council, law enforcement, and other, regarding the woman's behaviour.</u>

A seperate incident, involving the screaming woman, had occurred during the 5 years, and the <u>police were called</u> (by a different neighbour). Shamu, her husband, and a close friend of their's, <u>were all seen laughing resembling a scene underlying that they were long-time friends.</u>

Attempt offender profiling of Shamu:

-what is the offence/s?

-what is the concomitant offence?

-in which type of offending category does Shamu fit?

What are the alternatives to the local police, assuming that Shamu will continue with her current behaviors?

DEPARTMENTAL CORRUPTION: Case of Subterfuge; Disappearance; and False identity:

Curbie, was a <u>young child</u> who was <u>presumed to have been taken by a perpetrator.</u>

His <u>family of 5 siblings</u> seemed less disturbed than one would expect, regarding the child's disappearance.

Curbie, the <u>6 yo child</u> was <u>allegedly dropped (apparently accidently) on a train line</u> in the northern part of the state, and presumed dead.

Because the family had <u>departmental links</u>, this appears highly relevant:

the family, though appeared concerned, did not resemble a family with grief laden reactions.

All remained quiet, and the extended family did not dare mention the horrible incident which reportedly occured, resulting in the child's apparent death.

Literally, <u>8 years later, a young adolescent</u> (presented as a family friend), Antud, turned up: he was 14 years of age. He was embraced by the family, and the extended family, as a full member.

The name-sake of the adolescent (and that of the concomitant deceased child) came into question.

<u>It was presumed (by the extended family, and confirmed upon genealogical records) that the child (who was presumed/presented as deceased) was indeed the adolescent who presented before them.</u>

In the USA, the Lindbergh Law (Federal Kidnapping Act) exists. It surpasses state jurisdictions.

Which laws likewise exist in your region?

What is typically used as forensic evidence, for child abduction, child endangerment, and child kidnapping?

What is typically used in forensics, to identify hiding of a child and presenting them as missing or deceased?

What are your child custody laws like in your state, or country?

Attempt (by hand) to create a 'Photokit' (facial composite, much like the old form-Penry) of someone you know:

-be sure to include all essential facial features in order to assist in accurate identification.

CRIMINAL OFFENDING: Profiling

In traditional criminal profiling, there are 2 main categories of offenders: <u>the organized criminal; and, the disorganized criminal.</u>

The <u>Organized offender</u> typically has a planned life and, his/her criminal offending is triggered by a serious life event. He/she has high intelligence; holds a job; performs her/his criminal acts with premeditation and arrives at the scene with weapons; has controlled behavior during the crime; and, usually his/her victim is not personally known to the offender.

The <u>Disorganized offender,</u> on the other hand, undertakes his criminal acts usually in a form of crime of passion; with nil premeditation. He/she tends to leave more evidence at the crime scene/s.

He/she is often unemployed; socially inept; has limited IQ; and, typically a 'loner'.

The similarity between the 2 categories are that they both tend to revisit their crime scene, after the fact- though, with varying behaviors and with different levels of carefulness.

The <u>2 main approaches to criminal profiling:</u> are the <u>top-down</u>, whereby the criminal investigators start with large details; and the <u>bottom-down</u> approach, whereby small details are focussed upon firstly and build to a bigger picture.

The <u>bottom-up approach</u> (used often in Britain) utilises alot of digitalisation (as in, data mining). The data is explored to match certain criminal characteristics, with the typology that a criminal's characteristics remain constant in and out of a crime scene. The alleged offender/s knowledge of local geography/location awareness is a key component.

Please read the following:

Daffyd, is a 50 y.o. male, who has matriculated from high school and has completed training as an electrician. He is employed by a technological firm. Daffyd is married with 2 children, and 1 adopted child. He has a history of perpetrating psychological, and other forms of, abuse upon his wife, and enjoys giving his wife 'frights'; is controlling and is generally known as a 'know-it-all'; though, he has no history of childhood behavioral problems. He has shown paranoid tendencies since the age of 35 years; has never said the word 'sorry' in his life, and is proud of it; has a high IQ; constantly (approximately 50 times per day)
visits his shed on his urban property to check that all his tools are there; and becomes aggressive when he loses control over family members, friends and situations.

Daffyd is highly aware of police/law enforcement processes.

Daffyd became a suspect in the physical and mental torture, kidnapping, and extortion, of a 43 year old woman, for a period of 4 months.

He is considered a suspect, by the federal police, as his fingerprints were matched to one of the scenes of the crime.

Apply profiling techniques in regards to this alleged offender.

At the minimum decide:

-whether Daffyd is an organized, or disorganized, criminal?

at the maximum- whether he is:

-beyond an alleged/actual offender in the case of the 43 y.o. woman (or were his fingerprints present by happenstance. That is- was he coincidentally present before the offences took place, at the scene of the crime)?

-underline the key elements above; and,

-provide your reasons for your decision making, and conclusions.

-analyse your approach, was it more bottom-up or top-down? (did you focus on the alleged offence and work backwards?; or did you focus on the specifics then hone in on what has been alleged?)

SOCIAL MEDIA: Revenge; Hate crime/s; Bias crime--> Shared group mentality-->Lynch-mobbing (Targetting of 1/> individual/s)-->Impact of Lies--> Assault on Reputation-->Development of cultism

Narcissistic seduction: is the first step in cult recruitment. It is dependant upon: age; social presence; sense of family/desire for belonging; identity change/ formation of a promised solidification of identity; and, dependancy on group/ extreme socialism.

Misdirected vigilante justice, which often leads to development of cultism in the social media world, involves: organized groups filled with persons devoid of true identity/no identity formation who have a need for acceptance and, a blessed outlet for projection of anger and bitterness.

Addiction problems are closely aligned with this. Addictive disorders' criteria is closely linked with development of cultist thinking: "behavior, that can function both to produce pleasure and to provide escape from internal discomfort"
(6).

All of the above can lead to the gamification of learned hate; the acquiescence to mind control; the playing out of hypnotic and seductive lies; a feeling of group superiority; undoubtable indoctrination; the experience of supremacy; malleability for even more deleterious role modelling; promotion of continued propaganda via inauthenticity of information; and subjugation to desired authoritarianism.

Cate is an individual target. People posing on behalf of the green movement, lgbtqi, extreme socialists, mainstream religious groups, and disenchanted persons (nouveau religio-cultural and, other) perpetrate upon Cate- who is a victim of relentless threats, intimidation, slander, libel, defamation, malice, hatred, dangerous lies resulting not just in psychological harm but serious physical harm.

The perpetration is undertaken via social media, or social media apps.

The mode of operation, is essentially: vacillation of lies, and continue to be spread/trolling via social media, with some boasting that several social media contact modes are encrypted and thus are immune to different countries (and regional) data laws.

The lies vacillate from the person being called: a 'whore'; a non-disclosed transgender person; a criminal; a terrorist; that they are lying about their race and socio-cultural background to the point that even there country of origin is doubted; false religious/not beliefs.

From this, to being accused of making up their accreditations, professional accomplishments, career history, and academic qualifications; accusations and false representations that the victim is 'acting', with their reactions and answers not considered real.

Erasure of history of family members; countries visited; reducing the victim to a non-person with nil history, nil physicality (even when they are very physically sick), nil feelings, nil right to pursue goals, and nil chance of ever escaping the horrific vicissitudes.

Ultimately, a 'thing' to be ridiculed, laughed at endlessly, and denied every right to exist.

That the lies spread to people, not posing as in the first sentence, is a given. Seemingly innocent people are then drawn into the lies, join in and repeat similar behaviors to the original perpetrators.

Stalking, and inciting like-minded cultists to speak to the person face to face.

To taunt, to psychologically manipulate, to insult, to deride, and to reduce to below animal status, is part of their modus operandi.

When the victim attempts to talk to someone seemingly removed from 'the movement', she is then considered again a 'whore' (regardless of the gender of the person that they are attempting to speak with), or that the victim is acting/not real with the person in front of them and therefore using them. Invariably, the person never speaks with them again. Or worse, the victim inevitably sees the clear change toward them, as the turned-innocent become stand-offish, cold, and unapproachable.

This can continue for years, across multiple regions, and by people with/without allegiances with traditional social media outlets.

Part of the aim is to change the person, to traumatise them outright-yes, but to mould them into what the group wants. This changes from day to day, with extensive victimisation. So the victim, even in attempts to be compliant so it will 'just stop', always gets it wrong, never being allowed to understand what is right and wrong to please the ever-growing group.

The victim also has no privacy, peace, or given respect for any decision they make.

A <u>hostage situation</u> to say the least, but with no chance/capacity to try to identify with the hostage taker because it is impossible to pinpoint who is dominating the conversations of lies at a given point.

It is possible, nevertheless, in some circumstances, for the victim to <u>wind her/his mind back</u> to the <u>origins </u>of the victimisation and pinpoint the original perpetrator (the one most <u>intent on creating such hatred, horror, and attempts at sending the victim mad).</u>

The victim is <u>forever changed, not for the better.</u> However, they understand better than their offenders, the desire for <u>retribution, </u>along life-long, relentless avenues .

Especially if their life has been <u>decimated in every possible way.</u>

How have you encountered social media and the impact on healthcare workers' clinical decision-making?

Examine mistakes made in, eg hospital settings whereby- hearsay/access to social media about persons, certain groups- where resultant misidentification of a patient's characteristics comes into play?

With resultant medical errors emerge the realisation of forensic evidence retainment needed.

This can include:

-retaining the actual data

-vehicle of site access

-information on who accessed the site first

-details regarding date, time, and the decision making influencing information accessed

Describe the protocols in place for this to be efficiently undertaken.

MAINSTREAM CRIME: Assault: Sexual; Physical

Hilda, suffered a <u>near fatal knife wound</u>: she received deep lacerations from sternum to groin by her <u>partner of 5 years</u>.

She had many unresolved medical problems following the assault.

She had been <u>raped</u> repeatedly over a period of years, but also at the time of the near fatal assault.

The partner, following the assault, had also set part of Hilda's <u>house on fire.</u>

The victim spoke English well, but was deemed to need an interpreter, for court.

She was very traumatised, and emotionally fragile.

She had also been <u>threatened</u>, as she had no other alternative other than to remain in the <u>same house</u> where the assaults occurred.

Following the assaults, she had heard strange knocking at her doors and windows (at night) and had suffered several unsuccessful <u>house break-ins.</u>

She was offered <u>no protection</u>, and this continued for <u>several years</u> post-assault, regardless of the fact that the perpetrator had <u>threatened vengeance</u> and further assaults upon her, if she sought help following the near fatal attack.

Fortunately, in this case, the police statement was forwarded to the public prosecutor's office and a meeting between the public prosecutor's lawyer, the victim, the counsellor, and the interpreter, was undertaken.

All seemed to be going well with the case, until (after 2 months) the public prosecutor lawyer suddenly <u>disappeared</u>. The lawyer had left the country, and shortly after- the case was dropped.

The victim, and the counsellor, were not informed of this for a period of over <u>9 months</u>. So, the victim had continued to prepare herself, psychologically and emotionally, for court and had fortuitously dealt with the mental and physiological anguish involved in being placed in a high risk situation because of (what she believed was:) the pending court process.

Further, to the evidence, it was later discovered that the attending medical staff (at the time of emergency response to the near fatal attack) had <u>forgotten</u> to take photographs of the extensive injuries incurred.

The following is only the least of what needs to be collected (often by healthcare staff, depending upon the efficiency of law enforcement response).

With your knowledge/initial research, are there more considerations, than those listed below:

-photography, documentation: victim's injuries

-the retainment of the victim's clothing (without contamination)

-rape kit process undertaken (connected with protocols, also to be maintained for forensic evidence)

The attending healthcare workers may also need to write a forensic report.

What are the essential components of such?

Additionally, the medical history of the victim is important.

Which historical categories take precedence, in a case like this?

MAINSTREAM CRIME: Homicides

> *Homicide can take all forms, perpetrated by: groups of assailants/gangs; early released mentally unwell perpetrators; and, via organised crime.*

Mani, a 47 y.o. male, was set upon by a group of 7 assailants.

They were allegedly unknown to the victim.

One, at least, of the perpetrators, was newly released from a psychiatric institution-conditionally.

The crime was perceived (by police) as drug deal vengeance.

The victim was murdered by gunshot after being chased down on an urban street on a weekend day.

The emergency responders were phoned by an unknown caller, and gathered the following details:

-the assailants were apparently loud and appeared unhindered (according to the last known words stated by the victim)

-most residents in the very long main street (frequented by much traffic) were home, yet, no one heard.

Upon law enforcement requests, for many months, no witnesses came forward.

Access what you have learned about the criminal profiling process, your previous knowledge, and/or what you have learned about your power to assess criminal offending, and explain your understandings, of:

-the duties of the receiving emergency personnel post-crime scene?

-dealing with homicide victim family members?

Please list, in order of importance, the factors involved in approaching/treating homicide family member victims; and,

-what is the impact upon healthcare workers, in this regard?

What is your role (as healthcare worker, or allied law enforcement officer) when witnesses (who may come forward much later post-offence; or disclose to a healthcare worker having witnessed/heard the offence) emerge?

-create a list of internal contacts, and external contacts (where known) to access, in a case like this (eg witness/victim support persons).

INSTITUTIONAL POWER BASED CRIME:
Religious Movements

Institutional power based: religious (stalking, shunning, public shaming, can be typically utilised by, for example: NRMs; Jehovah's Witnesses; Opus Dei, Scientology)

> *-disfellowshipping; 'us and them'; use of specific language/code words/words to increase indoctrination, and much more, are relevant to such sects, and movements.*

Fortunately, and respectively, unfortunately, CAN: Cult Awareness Network (started in USA) was the first of its kind; until, the Church of Scientology bought the rights to the name.

Essentially, potential members are attracted (to the above groups) because of the following characteristics: disenfranchisement; aberrancy; attachment; accord; and moral superiority.

JWs are considered separatist/sectarian versus Catholics being considered as non-stigmatised and therefore non-separatist. However, Opus Dei is not considered part of mainstream Catholicism (it is a personal prelature), and thus- is separatist along with JWs, and Scientologists (and NRMs).

All 3 use stalking, shunning, disfellowshipping, and public shaming, as a consequence to leaving- which many have argued constitutes cult status, as it compromises international human rights' laws.

Perhaps the following example can extrapolate further:

Muire attended an <u>opus dei school </u>for several years.

Muire <u>did not partake in the after school </u>activities (termed 'retreats', but involved

examination of conscience activities- with a lay person/numerary, latin mass, and further

religious guidance with view to becoming a numerary).

When Muire left the school, along with many others in the class (more than half of the

class left, that particular year)--she was the <u>only one </u>who <u>re-entered the mainstream</u>

<u>Catholic school system-</u> despite the rest of the students being devoutly catholic (this was a

specific choice though unexplained, made both by the students and their

parents).

People from the mainstream (receiving) school were naturally concerned about

indoctrination and were initially wary of the student (Muire).

Murie <u>maintained contact with only one student</u> from her (opus dei school) class- yet, at

least <u>10 of the 14 students happened to 'bump into her'</u> (in non local areas, and places of

great distance from their homes).

Murie found this a little strange, but as she had made her views about opus dei known

(that she did not want to be part of it, nor was she ever a part of it, aside from

attending the school), she thought it must be just multiple strange coincidences.

When the appearances <u>started impacting her work life</u>, she began to become concerned.

That is, especially the <u>extensive period of time</u> over which these coincidences continued to

take place.

Meanwhile, the local church which her next of kin attended (who was also not an opus dei sympathiser, nor member) started employing priests from opus dei.

This was not made known until many years later. The initiation: <u>a teacher</u> <u>(from the opus dei school)</u> who travelled 20 kms from her residence to attend the church multiple times per week in a large urban city (for many many years), from the year that the student left the school.

<u>Sometimes it is possible that it is not a small world, it is something more concerning indeed...</u>

Counsellors, in particular, need to be aware of the impact of some religious groups, sub-groups, sects, and cults, before they heroically make statements about assessment outcomes, or provide a final diagnosis, for their client/s.

-Which components, are relevant to the above point?

In issues of protection, when physical danger is present:

-How do you make contact with/speak with law enforcement agency personnel regarding client/patient protection?

INSTITUTIONAL POWER BASED CRIME: Political

Gordani, an adolescent female who was <u>technologically savvy</u> attended for counselling.

She had alleged suffering <u>abuse</u> at the hands of a <u>direct family member</u>.

Many counselling sessions had taken place, when the adolescent suddenly announced

that the <u>perpetrator</u> was in fact in a <u>mainstream political party</u>.

The counsellor wondered why this information was <u>withheld for so long</u>.

Part of the counselling involved <u>writing reports</u> to access further sessions for the client.

Two reports had already been submitted, with perpetrator details included.

The accessing of reports was via a <u>public department</u>.

The counsellor became <u>concerned for both the safety</u> of their client, as well as the possible

impact upon themselves, as counsellor and writer of the reports.

What happens when confidentiality is limited?

The case would have gone to a victims of crime tribunal, what are the important evidential factors which should be noted in such a report?

DISCLOSURE/ WHISTLEBLOWING: Endemic Abuse

High profile cases of victims of crime of endemic abuses, homicides, or severe cases of assault, whereby the media (via media court representatives) have reported on the case from start of court proceedings to the time of the perpetrators' gaol sentences, are considered controversial and one would expect that the victims would naturally be treated with greater respect.

This is not necessarily the case, when it comes to mandatory police reporting to victims when their perpetrators are due for release from gaol.

In fact, it can sometimes go the other way- possibly an avoidance of further media attention- and dodging the focus of the perpetrators' early release without adequate protective barriers (such as witness protection) being offered to the victims.

It is understandable, then, if the victim does become aware of the perpetrators' pending/post release, that they return to the media outlet which covered the case to start with.

What are the pros and cons of media representation of high profile victims of crime cases?

In the event that you are a counsellor who is referred one (or many) high profile cases, and that this is made known to you- upon referral, how (if so) would you handle the client differently?

Which kinds of protection are in place for healthcare workers, and allied health workers, when media becomes focussed on one (or more) of their clients?

What would you do if you found out that one of your work colleagues had approached the media on a client's behalf?

What would you do if you found out that one of your work colleagues had been approaching a media company on their own behalf, for perverse incentivisation/ payment (and had gained the information from files, or by accessing tapes of counselling sessions)?

DISCLOSURE/ WHISTLEBLOWING: Healthcare Abuse

Beulah was an 80 y.o. <u>supposedly with a diagnosis of dementia</u> living in a high care needs section of a 3 tiered nursing home.

She had <u>significant weight loss</u>, but maintained her existing weight, she took a long time to eat the pulverised food which the <u>understaffed nursing carers fed her.</u>

She was incontinent of urine, and sometimes of faeces.

She <u>did not speak but made noises like 'bub, bub'</u>, and managed to communicate effectively with differing intonations of such.

She was unable to walk as her <u>muscles had atrophied</u> from the lengthy periods of sitting in a chair. One nurses' aide started to notice Beulah's style of communicating, that she <u>had a far better understanding</u> of what was being said to her, that her memory for recent events was quite clear.

Upon researching, the nurses' aide discovered that there was a <u>significant link between dementia like symptoms and that of institutionally-induced depression.</u>

The nurses' aide spent some time with Beulah, beyond shifts, and started introducing different ways of <u>stimulating Beulah's memory</u> (short-term and long-term), conversing with her.

What she discovered was inspiring. Beulah <u>started communicating in coherent words </u>(not mimicked but random) and <u>short sentences; she started feeding herself; and responding to time related questions.</u>

One day the nurses' aide (who only worked part-time at the nursing home) arrived after a 5 day absence to discover that Beulah had a <u>black eye</u>.

This was deemed to be because Beulah had <u>changed her behaviors</u>, and one of the other nurses (unknown, but reported) was not happy with Beulah being <u>compliant but more independant.</u>

A classic case of abuse on many levels.

Please consider the following:

What first comes to mind for mandatory reporting, in this case?

There is the issue of internal disclosure, to reduce further risk to the patient, and to other patients in the residential facility. What factors are intrinsic to this?

In an ideal situation, the police would have been called.

Which factors, as a healthcare service provider, would be necessary to collate to help police identify the final physical assault- offender (black eye)?

DISCLOSURE/ WHISTLEBLOWING:

Paedophile Rings

In recent years, there has been much focus upon absolute facts that the mainstream Catholic church (in particular)- as opposed to focus upon deviations of such, like personal prelatures, have hidden historical child sexual abuse and catholic clergy paedophile rings.

From the royal commission into: institutional responses to child sexual abuse conducted in Australia (in 2013-2017), to revelations made in Germany, along with a papal response, the amount of catholic church child abuse sufferers, and survivors, is breathtakingly grave.

However, the facts only become known when brave survivors (or family of those who have not survived) come forward to the relevant authorities.
It is then dependant upon the authorities to handle the cases; the victim statements made; and, information provided, in an honest, unencumbered, and non-corrupted way.

Thus, it remains in question as to whether several (or more) paedophile rings of this nature have been fully infiltrated and exposed.

Take the example, below:

Alan, a 48 y.o. male discloses to a healthcare worker that he has been <u>a victim of childhood sexual assault, by several priests, and brothers.</u>

This occurred when he was <u>attending school,</u> and spanned a period of 4 years.

The offenders included <u>visiting priests and brothers</u> (from outside the diocese) who were connected to the same <u>Brotherhood.</u>

At 47 y.o, Alan had <u>reported the abuse to the police, provided multiple police statements,</u> but had yet to hear from the <u>public prosecutor's office</u> as to whether the statements would be taken further.

Meanwhile, Alan was beside himself because he had recently discovered (after being told that 2 of the perpetrators were deceased) that <u>2 of the brothers are currently working in a school</u> connected by Brotherhood, at a distance of 40 kilometres from the site of the perpetration upon himself (some 30 plus years, earlier).

The healthcare worker wanted to help, however, because of the closed nature of such cases, was unable to provide much information (aside from the law enforcement, and mandatory reporting, processes).

This <u>case is not unique</u>, and in some countries <u>have not been exposed</u>, inspite of lengthy public inquiries.

What would you do, as a healthcare worker, if you were aware that mandatory reporting had failed to yield any response to perpetrators continuing to work with children/adolescents, in exactly the same types of settings where previous offending had occurred?

Further to this, what avenues would you explore, when you are aware that police statements from the victim (or victims) had been 'buried', and thus, the information would not be utilised, investigated, sent to upper levels of law enforcement personnel, or forwarded to any inquiries?

Which methods would you undertake, specifically for Alan? As clinical healthcare worker? As counsellor? Or as social worker?

How would you investigate, and take action, if you were the receiving police officer in this case?

If you, as the receiving police officer was pressured by your colleagues, and upper management, to 'bury' the victim's police statements (because they are too controversial; or the paperwork is too burdensome), how would you handle the pressurisation?

Please provide specifics.

AVO: Apprehended Violence Order

DOJ: Department of Justice (USA)

DV: Domestic Violence

EMO: Emocore/Emotional Hardcore

EU: European Union

FOI: Freedom of Information

Goth: Gothic

IQ: Intelligence Quotient

JWs: Jehovah Witnesses

NRMs: New Religious Movements

UN: United Nations

REFERENCES

1) United Nations (1985), Declaration of basic principles of justice for victims of crime and abuse of power: adopted by General Assembly resolution 40/34 of 29 November 1985, United Nations: 1-3

2) UK Ministry of Justice (2005): Domestic violence, crime and victims act 2004: Victim's code, the code of practice for victims of crime, www.legislation.gov.uk>

3) Official Journal of the European Union (2012), Directive 2012/29/EU of the European Parliament and of the Council of 25 October 2012: establishing minimum standards on the rights, support and protection of victims of crime, and replacing Council Framework Decision 2001/220/JHA, L315/63:56.

4) Official Journal of the European Union (2012), Directive 2012/29/EU of the European Parliament and of the Council of 25 October 2012: establishing minimum standards on the rights, support and protection of victims of crime, and replacing Council Framework Decision 2001/220/JHA, L315/58:16.

5) Official Journal of the European Union (2012), Directive 2012/29/EU of the European Parliament and of the Council of 25 October 2012: establishing minimum standards on the rights, support and protection of victims of crime, and replacing Council Framework Decision 2001/220/JHA, L315/65:66.

6) Goodman, A. (1990), Addiction: definition and implications, Br.J.Addict 85(11), 1403-1408.

REFERENCES

1) United Nations (1985), Declaration of basic principles of justice for victims of crime and abuse of power: adopted by General Assembly resolution 40/34 of 29 November 1985, United Nations: 1-3

2) UK Ministry of Justice (2005): Domestic violence, crime and victims act 2004: Victim's code, the code of practice for victims of crime, www.legislation.gov.uk>

3) Official Journal of the European Union (2012), Directive 2012/29/EU of the European Parliament and of the Council of 25 October 2012: establishing minimum standards on the rights, support and protection of victims of crime, and replacing Council Framework Decision 2001/220/JHA, L315/63:56.

4) Official Journal of the European Union (2012), Directive 2012/29/EU of the European Parliament and of the Council of 25 October 2012: establishing minimum standards on the rights, support and protection of victims of crime, and replacing Council Framework Decision 2001/220/JHA, L315/58:16.

5) Official Journal of the European Union (2012), Directive 2012/29/EU of the European Parliament and of the Council of 25 October 2012: establishing minimum standards on the rights, support and protection of victims of crime, and replacing Council Framework Decision 2001/220/JHA, L315/65:66.

6) Goodman, A. (1990), Addiction: definition and implications, Br.J.Addict 85(11), 1403-1408.